DADDY DRINKS COFFEE

POPS & HOPS
PUBLISHING

DADDY DRINKS COFFEE

Author: M. T. Resh

Illustrator: Steven Kernen

Text and Illustration Copyright © 2020 Pops & Hops Publishing

All rights reserved. No part of this publication may be reproduced, distributed, or transmitted in any form or by any means, including photocopying, recording, or other electronic or mechanical methods, without the prior written permission of the publisher or author, except in the case of brief quotations embodied in critical reviews and certain other non commercial uses permitted by copyright law.

ISBN : 978-1-7342071-0-1 (Paperback)
978-1-7342071-1-8 (eBook)

TO EMERSON "MY NUGGET":

I would not trade my sleepless nights with you for all of the coffee in the world!

Love,
 Your Daddy who drinks lots and lots of coffee!

DADDY DRANK COFFEE

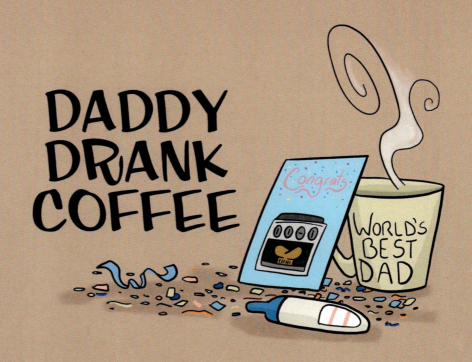

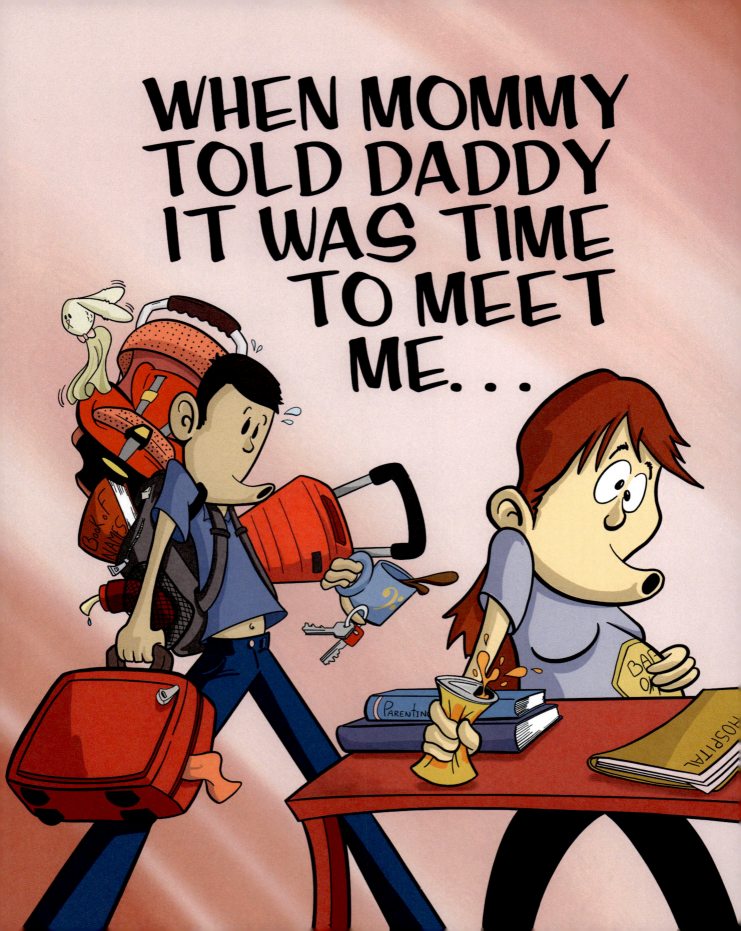

WHEN WE ARE DRIVING PLACES AND PEOPLE IN OTHER CARS DO NOT USE TURN SIGNALS, DADDY LOOKS REALLY MAD AND THEN...

WHEN POLITICS COME ON THE TELEVISION SCREEN, DADDY TURNS THE CHANNEL AND THEN...

BEANS OF ENCOURAGEMENT FOR DADS EVERYWHERE:

Hang in there new dads as life will get easier day by day or at least your coffee will get stronger and stronger!

The many diaper changes, spit up messes, and sleep deprivation will all be worth it in the end as your little one smiles back at you and helps create a "new normal" for you and your family in terms of your daily routine.

There is no greater title you can hold than being called "Dad" and your little one is very lucky to have you!

So as you hold the title of dad, be sure to hold a delicious cup of coffee and enjoy every moment, taking mental pictures along with real ones as your new wonderful life unfolds.

-Cheers and best of luck!

Author M. T. Resh is an avid coffee drinker of all sorts of beans but prefers medium roast java to start off his day on the left foot. He is a proud papa to his daughter Emerson and his Goldendoodle Elle, sips his morning cup of coffee alongside his beautiful wife Kayla, and works as an elementary school counselor in Lancaster, PA. M. T. Resh has authored previous books "Dneirf" and "Cardinal Connection" and loves to write and create fun stories that offer a 'learning undercover" experience for his readers.

Illustrator Steven Kernen enjoys one part coffee to three parts creamer. While the caffeine rush is good, he gets his natural high from his wife and two children . . . and the smell from his markers. Mmmmmmmm. . . markers.

Maybe I should open a window.

Made in the USA
Monee, IL
05 March 2020